Hayes, West Wickham and Keston

in old picture postcards

by
Muriel V. Searle

European Library – Zaltbommel/Netherlands

Acknowledgements

The author makes grateful acknowledgement to all who have loaned postcards additional to her own collection, or have given permission to reproduce them, especially: Jill Baldwin, ENBRO (Environment Bromley), Don Frisby, Irene Searle, Mr. G.W. Smith, May Stevens, Raphael Tuck Ltd.

After up to 85 years the original publishers have almost all proved untraceable, including those whose pictures were only copies of copies. However, thanks are given to those originally inscribed by name: A.E. Series, Christian Novels Series, D.B.L. Series, W.H. Drake, Earle Bromley, Enright Series, C.W. Faulkner & Co., Fields Kent Series, Friths Series, Grange Publishing Co., Hartmann Series, S. Hildesheimer, L.L. Series, Marshall Keene & Co., Milton Glazette, P.S. & V., B. Purdy Keston Post Office, S.F.S. Series, Tanners Photo Series, W.A.F. Series, B.C. Waters, Woolstone Bros.

GB ISBN 90 288 4694 8 / CIP

INTRODUCTION

Maps from only about 130 years ago (a mere four or five generations back) show Bromley as a little market town, starting at the historic College and ending about where is now the Churchill Theatre. Even so, it was considered to be of some importance, by virtue of its Bishops' Palace, its market, then of some seven centuries' standing, and its position on the main road to Tunbridge Wells and the Kent ports; the first stage outside London for changing horses.

Having such relative importance, it naturally had a ring of smaller satellites, equivalent to suburbs, whose names today are merely identifications for parts of a big town which are completely indistinguishable from the general sweep of urban development: Plaistow, Farwig, Southborough, Bickley, Widmore, Sundridge, and eventually the much later New Bromley. All of them were then separated by open countryside, or the spreading Palace estates. Today the notion of walking across fields to somewhere as close as Farwig seems inconceivable.

A second ring of satellite villages lay further out, between about two and five miles away, but were still tied up with Bromley for trade (a market for their farm produce and simple manufactures) and for support of human life (for shopping, medicine and entertainment). They included places like Hayes, West Wickham, Keston, Farnborough, Orpington and Beckenham. The latter two were swallowed whole by Bromley during the great 1930s suburb-building boom, linked into one continuous sprawl of modern residential roads, their old village centres pulled down for building the parades of largely all-alike new shops required by the residents of the new all-alike roads and avenues. Not to mention the addition of cinemas and new public houses.

The major factor encouraging this swift and all-embracing transformation of village into suburb was Southern Railway electrification, making what we now call commuting so quick and cheap that living in semi-country while working in London was more practicable than ever before for ordinary young husbands with mortgages. For their grandfathers' generation, living in places like Farnborough while working in Town was initially the prerogative mainly of big businessmen with private carriages to ferry them over to Beckenham or Bromley to travel First Class to their board rooms.

Now there were the new trains, and with them came a new demand for more modest houses in the £400 to £650 bracket and a £25 deposit, which every speculative builder in the district was more than ready to cash in upon. Directly the mortgage agreements were signed, the next two fields were bought from farmers equally willing to cash in; within a few years the countryside was gone.

However, several others of the former outlying villages stood, and mercifully still stand, between rural and urban states, again largely for railway reasons. Hayes and West Wickham acquired the advantage of their own branch line's electrification, but the operative word was 'branch'; a little quiet terminus instead of a main line rushing through linking everyone with everywhere; a useful but specifically local route. Suburbanisation certainly came to them both, but it had an outer limit instead of sweeping on and on. They were linked up in the railway's vicinity to places like Shirley and Elmers End, but to the south were very noticeably less developed. Today there is still this same dual character to both Hayes and West Wickham; archetypal Thirties suburbs where suburbia suddenly stops, in the same places where it stopped in the Thirties; behind the houses on such roads as Corkscrew Hill spread the same miles of rolling Kent/Surrey border country over which they looked when newly built.

Thirdly, there were the villages that remained more truly villages, albeit with a modicum of new roads. Again because of railways or, rather, lack of railways. Had all the schemes and dreams for lines into Farnborough and Keston materialised, they would probably now be, at worst, another Penge, at best another Petts Wood. In the event, trains passed them by; not least because the hilly terrain making this countryside so beautiful would also have made it expensive to engineer; even by Victorian standards the number of cuttings and, possibly, tunnels required would have made such ideas as linking Lewisham, Bromley and Croydon cross-country prohibitively expensive compared with possible passenger use. As a result, they are still in essence country villages; in Keston's case, complete with windmill, ponds, and sweeps of gorse and heather, that could be the other end of the world from London, or even modern Bromley or Croydon.

All these one-time villages (urban, suburban and rural) were copiously portrayed on the picture postcards whose heyday ran from about the time of Edward VII's accession to just after the Second World War, when the telephone became virtually universal in private homes. Previously, postcards performed the same function, conveying simple messages from person to person. Mailbox clearances and house deliveries were as a result so frequent that a card saying simply 'Will be over to tea this afternoon' could be posted at breakfast time, received soon after lunch, and the table be laid when the visitors arrived. Every uneventful triviality for which we would pick up the phone was conveyed by picture postcard; so necessary were they, therefore, that mothers often kept a number always in a handy drawer, ready for dashing off for the price of a ha'penny stamp.

The card itself might have cost one old penny (⅓p). Today they are collector's fair items, at antique prices. The addition of a few market stalls or a policeman on horseback may push the cost of a one-time penny postcard to £10, or even more. The ability of dealers to demand, and get, such prices, stems from the universal law of supply and demand. No longer a means of sending family messages, they have become transformed by time into invaluable mirrors of the past. One of the best means of building up a very complete picture of how one's own area looked in great-grandfather's day.

This was the period when any place was changing faster than ever before; the cards he and his family sent therefore show so many scenes that were quickly to vanish for ever. Every bit of background is important to we who now collect local cards; the buses, trams, butcher boys' delivery cycles, dairymen's milk-carts, shop advertisements on the walls. They are the pieces of social history that give life and meaning to the actual settings, which have themselves also often since changed beyond recognition. Small wonder that collectors' fairs limited entirely to old postcards, some of them featuring fifty or more dealers with huge stocks, attract buyers from many miles around, each looking for one more piece in the jigsaw that is the history of his own town, willing to pay more for one card that he badly needs than the person who penned it would have earned in a working week. The author quite recently (albeit grudgingly) paid £12 for a scence featuring her grandfather's old shop premises in Bromley; exactly his pay for managing the same business for a month. Was it worth it? Intrinsically, no; it was still only a penny postcard, and none too clean. Historically, yes; it was the first time she had ever actually seen what the shop looked like, the kind of stock it sold; the window dressed with his own hands. That is the fascination of postcard collecting. Above all, if one's interest is an area like this, on the dividing line between age-old countryside and ever-changing twentieth century suburbia.

June 1988   Muriel V. Searle

15667 HAYES LANE & CHURCH.

1. Horse transport through an otherwise deserted Hayes, long before addition of the present shops and houses. The church was therefore still the centrepiece, both visually and socially, periodically added to by parishioners who could afford to commemorate themselves or their families for future generations to remember. Two of the more recent donations were windows given in 1858. One, a resurrection scene, was given 'by the family of the late Samuel Neville Ward Esq., of Baston', and with a dedication 'to the memory of him and of his wife'. The other, also in the chancel, showed Christ healing the sick, but was more unusual in that those subscribing financially towards its installation were not publicly thanked by name; the local paper simply recorded that it was 'placed there by the Gentry of the Parish'.

Hayes Church.

2. Though largely rebuilt in 1880, St. Mary The Virgin at Hayes stands on a very hallowed site. A new church was built in about 1200, but presumably replaced an even older one, as the list of Rectors' names starts a quarter of a century before that date. Altered into the then fashionable Early English style in about 1400, it eventually went through the usual Reform period additions of a gallery and a towering pulpit to emphasise the great importance of the sermon. Three tiers tall, it ascended from the parish clerk, seated at ground level, to the presiding clergyman of the day in the middle, to the preacher himself on the top deck, with his hour-glass or sermon-glass measuring out his dissertation in trickling grains of sand. And it could well last a full hour, through to its interminable winding-up sequence of Fifthly, Sixthly, Finally, Lastly and In Conclusion. With the clerk and two clergy watching form this viewpoint, who dared fall asleep?

3. One of the strangest Pitt family stories about Hayes Church (seen here in about 1902) concerns the funeral of 'the great Lord Chatham' in Westminster Abbey, where the elaborate heraldic banners carried in the procession were afterwards hung on display. But later they came to the Pitts' own Hayes parish, where for about seventy years they hung gathering both historic interest and dust. Then they disappeared, never to be seen again. Popular hearsay believed that a house-proud (or, rather, church-proud) charlady, whose feeling for cleanliness was offended by their grubbiness every time she scrubbed the church, sneakily removed them and gave them decent burial, probably in her coal fired kitchen range. Luckily, pictorial reproductions existed, and in about 1920 Mrs. Torrens of the Crove presented a new banner copied from the old, to be hung over the chancel screen. It showed Lord Chatham's coat of arms between a lion and stag, with his coronet, and the motto 'Benigo Numine'.

4. An incalculable unwitting crime against local art was perpetrated at the George in Hayes. 'A quaint picturesque place (that) boasts of a remarkable public picture gallery, the sign of the George & Dragon being, it is said, an early painting by Sir J.E. Millais,' as was remarked in a guidebook of the 1890s. The 'picture gallery' was in fact just one painting, not in a museum but hanging outdoors in all weathers. The young Millais when visiting the George supposedly gave its landlord – possibly in lieu of cash, as was done in contemporary France by the impecunious Barbizon painters – a gift whose modern value would be in tens of thousands of pounds; a new sign specially painted, showing George with the dragon. A later publican unknowingly sent it to destruction by trying to preserve it, for by about 1875 it was only fit to be described as 'too much blackened to be made out'. Aware of its interest, and rather than trust a village artisan, he sent it for cleaning to a conceited minor Keston artist. The latter decided to do even better and update it. Millais' art was completely burned off, and replaced by a daub of his own!

5. A modest country hostelry, the New Inn as shown here bears no relationship to the present massive mock-medieval baronial hall, opposite Hayes station; an unusual and rather magnificent exercise in almost monastic splendour. This smaller and older New Inn, no more than a local beerhouse serving villagers, cyclists and ramblers, vanished in about 1935 when the great rush of incoming suburbia seemed to demand something more towny. The newer New Inn, still flourishing today, was erected by a Midlands brewery company, apparently in a fantasy style much favoured there, but unique in Kent. It was heavily damaged in the 1940 blitz and remained partly wrecked for several years – (and two men died in the raid) – but was restored to its massive glory in 1962.

Hayes Grove

6. Symmetrical Georgian elegance in Hayes Grove, whose formal grounds have unusual tree associations. One, a huge Cedar of Lebanon, is said to have been planted by a woman missionary, who left a similar permanent memento wherever she stopped to preach. Another, an English oak, allegedly commemorated the union of England with Scotland. Lady Baker Wilbraham, who once lived at Hayes Grove, before her marriage in 1930, was descended from Hayes forebears of two centuries before. After various wartime uses, the house became a rest home for invalid ex-nurses, bought for this purpose by King Edward's Hospital Fund and leased to the London Hospital for only nominal rent. This view appears to have been posted by a very old and infirm resident, as an Easter card.

7. One of the first motor buses trundles into Hayes on an otherwise deserted road. 'Outside only' meant just that: on top, outside under the wind and rain, huddled into blankets or waterproofs. Decades after top decks were covered in, busmen today still sometimes use this expression instead of the more logical 'On top only'. By this period, the 1920's buses were greatly improved on the skeletal services passing for a timetable in the early days of public transport. When trains came to Bromley, almost the only means of going on to the town's outskirts was by such routes as Fownes's Keston Omnibus, connecting with a mere handful of daily trains. From Keston in 1865, for example, they ran for the 9.54 and 10.43 am, or the 3.34 and 8.09 pm from Bromley to London, from the Red Cross. On Sundays, missing the 10.30 am bus, (which involved a long wait for the 11.54 am train) meant either waiting some nine hours for the next, or not travelling at all. The card is captioned 'Mary's Cottages, Hayes' and postmarked 1924.

8. Hayes gained its first Post Office, in Baston Road, in 1883; just one year after the railway came to herald its first steps towards modern development. About twenty years later this attractive postcard went on sale, showing a combined cake shop and Post Office, the shop being basically the largest front parlour of a cottage; much like Miss Sands' butchery of 1899, started in the front room of one of the nearby St. Mary's Cottages and very unusual in being run by a woman. Robert Pearce, the village postmaster, started in 1894; he worked right through to 1934, spanning the most dramatic and drastic period of residential development the place had ever seen. His first customers were villagers, every one known by name; his final ones were new suburbians, more distinguished by their numbers and their newness than as personal friends. A white-bearded Santa Claus, he was reckoned to have plodded the equivalent of four times around the world, on the lanes of Hayes, starting his first round at 6 am, and his last round thirteen hours later.

Hayes Village, Kent.

9. All manner of gifts were enclosed with popular magazines up to 1939, as a bait to attract further readers. Women's papers frequently gave away complete paper patterns for anything from a ballgown to a baby's christening robe; or short paperback novelettes. One series gave free picture postcards, distributed through a local newsagent and relating to his own area, again by way of publicity; they were the forerunners of the miniature perfumes or shampoo sachets sometimes now attached to front covers, to serve the same purpose. This card had a printed note on the back 'Given free... with Smart Novels, Yes & No, Dainty Novels, Weekly Tale Teller', showing a very rural corner of Hayes; one cottage appears to have a Regency period porch.

10. Picturesque and not exactly burdened with modern amenities like street lights, is Hayes as seen in about 1905; there is no sign of electricity, or even the 'few gas lamps' planned for the village in the 1880s. But at least it had acquired pavements, a great improvement on dust tracks in summer or mud in winter, always scattered with horse manure.

15664 HAYES POST OFFICE & VILLAGE.

11. Hayes village (population 621 at the 1871 census) had still not changed much when this postcard was mailed soon after the turn of the century, described in the 1870s as 'quiet and respectable, and chiefly dependent on the wealthy residents (with)... a few ordinary houses and shops'. It was approached from Bromley by 'a pleasant lane overhung with elms, with hop gardens, and wheat fields on either side'. Not quite like the route of the 119 bus! Hayes Place still existed, beloved of 'the great Lord Chatham' and birthplace of his even greater son, William Pitt. So bitterly did Pitt regret eventually selling it that he almost immediately began campaigning to buy it back. Today, the only outward sign of a pre-suburban past in that particular quarter is a very charming old lodge, incongruously fitting in between the inter-wars terraced villas facing the former Guernsey Farm.

12. Another version of the old Post Office area, from about 1910. A rather smart governess cart is conveying a well-dressed lady through Hayes, in the care of a substantially built top-hatted driver.

13. In postcards of almost any town or village, certain standardised scenes were repeated in many versions and variants, while others – such as Coney Hall – were scarcely touched. Hayes Post Office was a typical example of the first category, published from many viewpoints within the same short stretch of road. Here we have a slightly different one, in that the date may be a little later than most classic cards, judging by the tidied-up road and smart new fences, plus a couple of public signs. Posing outside is a village postman in uniform; the bigger and taller man in 'civvies' was presumably the postmaster himself.

14. Hayes Gate would have been a boundary between Hayes and Bromley, similar to one between Beckenham and Penge which also marked the division of Kent from Surrey. The busy highway now used as a racetrack by buses, cars and lorries, is here little better than a lane, cut deep down between grassy banks and used by just two people, one cart and one horse. However, a few fragments of the old order did linger surprisingly long. Well after the Second World War, one wooden shack bungalow survived among the new suburban villas, inhabited by an old sailor whose parrot spent all summer on a perch in the front garden. Another was the high lying land west of this road, known as the Cabbage Fields, crossed by footpaths from the top of Stone Road to Mead Way; the reek of rotting cabbages in autumn carried right across to the football ground in Hayes Lane. Both cabbages and countryside vanished under the present Hayesford Park estate, named from the almost forgotten Hayes Ford across an equally forgotten little stream. This card was on sale in 1905, but the picture itself is older, found previously in an 1894 local directory.

15. Dainty birches on Hayes Common, until the advent of universal private motoring one of the most popular places for local recreation. Bromley businesses of the early 20th century took their apprentices there by open horse-brake for summer outings, with simple races and buckets of lemonade. Croydon offices did the same for the annual staff treats. In the 1800s, without even this degree of mass transport, Hayes was popular within a shorter radius for its fairs, frolics and 'rustic gambols'. The latter spilled over from the village centre for such events as 'cricket to be play'd on Hays (sic) Common'. But even in late Victorian days the village was still so small as to have no direct mail deliveries, being brought from London via Bromley. But services improved in 1869 when it was announced that 'Beckenham has now been made head office for the district', supposedly ensuring the postman's appearance two hours earlier in the day.

16. The writer's father and aunt, as small children, playing in a deep sea of autumn leaves at Hayes Common in about 1910-1912. A private snapshot, but printed in postcard form, with a proper postcard backing, acceptable to be sent through the mail exactly like an ordinary commercial card.

On the Road to Hayes Common from Bromley.

17. Vaguely titled 'On the road to Hayes Common from Bromley', this picture may be what is now called Hayes Lane, where deep embankments were originally cut down to ease the passage of horse-drawn traffic. They still survive where the first fields open out, near the former Guernsey Farm. Hayes Guernsey Farm gave high quality milk, and the cows were until fairly recently a feature of the meeting point of suburbia and country. Golden coated, they were usually in the fields where market-garden or pick-your-own crops are nowadays raised, or waiting in the yard (which is still little altered) to be milked.

A CHARMING SPOT, HAYES COMMON

18. On the back of this 1908 view a more modern hand has added 'now psychiatric hospital in Prestons Road'.
In 1908 it was just an idyll of greenery looking a million miles from London – or even from burgeoning Bromley.

19. The cows come home, across the lonely Commons that are now crossed by motor roads, only a few years after the opening of the 20th century.

Hayes. Common.

20. A winter or very early spring view on Hayes Common, posted in May 1909. A black-and-white view, hand coloured for postcard reproduction. Usually both original and painted versions were on sale; the once-universal choice of 'penny plain, tuppence coloured'.

21. Streets and houses eternally change and are rearranged by men. Thankfully, the Commons do not, being in general arranged by Mother Nature. The overall character of this very early 20th century landscape is easily recognisable throughout the area today, off the roads.

22. The characteristic building method known to the Thirties as ribbon-development linked Bromley and Hayes, along Hayes Lane, whose appearance has not greatly changed since then. But behind those houses, where are now Hayesford Park and other modern roads, a whole stretch of country vanished after the Second World War. A child's surviving geography lesson survey from 1948 recalls now how most of Hayesford was then under crops. Not only the well-remembered cabbages, but wheat, turnips and market gardening, together with allotments. However, by then there were already large stretches of what the pupil called 'waste land, scrub etc'. In other words: fields no longer cropped and 'ripe for development'; earmarked for sale for housing. Changed in the Thirties, and about to change again in the Fifties, Hayes had by then already altered drastically since it consisted mainly of lonely cottages for making into romantic postcards.

BARNET WOOD LANE,
HAYES KENT.

23. Away from the roads, the local paths and commons today continue to abound in small wildlife. Even more so before housing took away so many fields. One can imagine the driver of this leisurely cart through Barnet Wood Road, soon after Edward VII came to the throne, hearing at first hand from his parents how Pokey Alley got its name. From the handsome if vicious polecats living in Polecat Valley, hence Polecat Alley, before Coney Hall became respectably suburbanised. Constricted though it is between semi-tamed hedges, even now Pokey Alley keep an aura of gloom and mystery, hemmed between almost oppressive walls of verdure.

24. Historic prints were commonly re-issued in postcard form, early in the twentieth century. Being a period of such swift developments in house building and in transport, villages that had remained fairly constant for centuries were changing before their residents' eyes. Already, it was hard to picture them only a couple of generations back. A scene like this (of the George at Hayes) was thus almost unbelievable to a person of King Edward VII's time; just as the village he then considered was becoming modern and spoilt looks unimaginably countrified to ourselves, again removed by two or three further generations.

The School and Village, Hayes

25. 'The school and village, Hayes' is the caption of an undated early 20th century view card. A forerunner school for forty pupils was built in 1791, with just two teachers, husband and wife. In 1865 the boys' and girls' classes were combined into one co-educational scheme. One headmaster, William Plant, taught here for just under fifty years, from 1874 to 1923; from the peak of Victorian empire-building, to the dawn of 20th century suburb-building.

26. One end of the lengthy Hayes Lane is firmly in Bromley (or, rather, Bromley Common), the other runs into Hayes itself, linking what were formerly a small country market town and an outlying village. The school now known as Ravensbourne, being in Hayes Lane, perhaps therefore qualifies for inclusion. Even now, its frontage overlooks open fields towards Hayes. An aerial view of about 1925 shows a complete lack of modern housing along the Lane, and a lot more open land behind the buildings. The great hall had not yet been added, but obviously the accommodation in general was already proving inadequate; a line of makeshift additional rooms can be seen at the left.

27. Ravensbourne's main hall has long acted as Bromley's concert hall, one of the few able to seat a full symphony orchestra, especially before the building of the Great Hall at Stockwell College (now the Civic Centre). By virtue of the Whyte sisters, for several decades the leading figures of Bromley Symphony Orchestra, virtually all the great musical names between the 1940s and 1970s appeared here, including Sir Adrian Boult, Sir George Dyson, Isobel Baillie, Heddle Nash, Paul Tortelier and Dennis Brain.

Hayes Grove.   *Hayes.*

28. On the surface, one would not associate such an innocent-looking village with hot politics. But in the same month that this postcard was sold (November 1907) a very heated political meeting indeed took place at the Swan, West Wickham, 'under the auspices of the Hayes District of the Conservative-Unionist Polling Association'. The issue was 'Tariff Reform... as an absolute necessity'. There was an almost dockyard-gate hotheadedness about the tendency to demand rather than suggest: 'The time would soon come when the working men would demand it and get it.'

29. St. Mary's Cottages, part of old pre-suburbanised Hayes, were part of the small huddled community centred on the church and the little village school. The latter, like most others, doubled out of lesson hours as a community centre, for such unassuming entertainments as displays by the Hayes Gymnastic Club. In the year that this view of St. Mary's Cottages was posted (1908) the Club numbered twelve senior and ten junior boys, plus some girls. Their latest display, according to the perhaps less than critical local magazine-cum-newspaper, 'would have been creditable to any club, rural or urban'.

30. 'Twixt Hayes and Keston' is the description of this romanticised sunset scene posted in 1908. A flock of sheep blocks a road that is today rather more heavily used, by motor traffic. A few years previously a local gazetteer had called this area of Hayes and Keston countryside 'one of the most charming bits of scenery in the whole of Kent'. On another page it repeated: 'The scenery in this district (is) exquisitely beautiful.' Both observations hold perfectly good today, off the main roads, especially when high banks of wild gorse turn the commons to flaming yellow in spring; or when great sweeps of heather create a miniature Scotland in August.

Baston Manor Corner, Hayes.

31. A mad rush of pioneer motor vehicles – all three of them (one at the crossroads, two in the distance). But local papers were full of things to come by the early 1930s, like the headline 'Too Much Noise' detailing imposition of a 10s (50p) fine to a Keston man for 'driving a motorcycle combination with excessive noise' through Bromley, and another 10s for 'not having proper wings and mudguards'. Threats to historic sites by road widening were already common; in 1932 the council were 'prepared to agree to the removal of Dr. Hussey's Well, New Road, Hayes… to a site on the new line of the road when widened'. Motoring small-ads were already proliferating; a nice Morris Tourer secondhand for £23, or mayby a Morris Cowley four seater for £20. What we might now term a banger, at the cheap end of the secondhand column, ranged from a Royal two seater for £7, to a cheap van sold off by a laundry at Lee. Significantly, the 'Horses, Stabling etc' column had by then shrunk to only two items (stables to let at 7s.6d (37½p) a week); soon it would be dropped completely.

Corner of Hayes Common.

32. Only one man is on the road, and too unbothered by traffic, if any, to walk near the fence. However, by this time (about 1905) a small modicum of public transport did cross the Commons. In about 1900 horse buses began running out from the White Hart at Bromley, and on to Keston. In 1914 a motor bus took over, all the way from Bromley to Downe, a forerunner of the still surviving 146 route. A solid-tyred bone-shaker, it was run by one Fred Capon; no inappropriate name for a man carrying the many locals who supplemented their meagre incomes by keeping poultry.

33. The utter emptiness of pre-mass-motoring Hayes. Except for the surfaced roads, instead of dirt tracks, it could almost pass for the different kind of loneliness that six centuries before stemmed from more than mere lack of human presence at a particular moment. Then, what few residents did exist, about 140 people in all, were almost exactly halved to a mere sixty-nine, by a terrifying visitation of plague. It seems to have taken two or three generations before natural sequences of marriage and birth among the survivors restored the village's previous level. Certainly enough grown men lived there in 1450 to supply a contingent for the famous Jack Cade Rebellion – a peculiarly Kentish affair – when two thousand marched to a still legendary rally on Blackheath.

ON HAYES COMMON, KENT.

AFTER THE ORIGINAL PAINTING BY S. JOHNSON

34. Junior employees and apprentices of nearby towns, like Bromley and Croydon, were often taken out to Hayes or Keston Commons for staff outings or half-day-off treats, especially between about 1910 and 1939. Their transport might well be by horse-brake; a boneshaking open vehicle with long sideways benches; instead of two by two. If the overburdened horse broke down or went lame – not infrequently – half the fun was having to walk the rest of the way, singing the latest music hall hits, with two strong men lugging the bucket of lemonade. Finding a clearing or open space like this one, they spent the afternoon running easy sports such as three legged, sack, or egg-and-spoon races, followed by picnic tea with the lemonade. Given motorways to take us farther in a half day they would have travelled for a fortnight's holiday, we also perhaps miss as much as we gain. The simplicity of an afternoon out, so near to home, is foregone in favour of a long and wearisome battle against the traffic jams to reach a very similar picnic site a hundred miles away; simply because it *is* a hundred miles away.

35. No sign of any car on the lonely road when somebody sent their card early in 1907. But had she walked there on 6th July it would have been amazingly different, as a largely horse-drawn world was invaded by Kent Automobile Club on its way to a Motor Gymkhana at Holwood Park. Rarely were so many of the newfangled horseless carriages seen together, as when the enthusiasts from all over Kent puttered and sputtered over the Commons: 'Cars of all shapes, sizes, and makes from a 6 hp De Dion to a 40 hp Mercedes... many of them painted in bright colours and occupied, in addition to the drivers, by ladies fashionably attired in the daintiest of summer costumes', according to a reporter who watched in amazement. The list of vehicles reads like a present-day veteran car lover's dream, including a 35 hp Rochet Schneider; a 15 hp Darracq; some 10-12 hp Argylls; a little 7-8 hp Swift; several more De Dions; and some 30 hp Humbers.

THE POND ON HAYES COMMON, KENT.

AFTER THE ORIGINAL PAINTING BY S. JOHNSON.

36. Various half hidden waters survive on the Commons, some dried up into mere hollows, others still flowing; notably the deeply hollowed one past which march the dozens of May Queens and their courts onto Hayes Common, on the final leg of their procession from the church. A few cottages like these also survive, but too often wedged between the modern houses that mushroomed all round them. Behind one group still can be seen the open drying-ground of the village washerwomen who lived there, taking in laundry from better-off ladies, which was dried on this communal airing place. Cottagers like those usually raised a few vegetables to feed their families cheaply, but some took much greater interest in horticulture, as members of Hayes Cottage Gardeners' Association. Their annual shows, started in about 1890, took place on meadows loaned by interested landowners, who also might supply the most expert judges in the district: the head gardeners of the great estates. Reports of the 1908 show, for instance, reveal that the judges were 'Mr. Whittle, gardener to Mr. Goschen of Croydon', Adams the gardener to Lord Avebury of the huge High Elms estate; and Rowbottom, Sir Henry Lennard's gardener from Wickham Court.

ON HAYES COMMON, KENT.

AFTER THE ORIGINAL PAINTING BY S. JOHNSON.

STANNARD

37. 'On Hayes Common, Kent': one child and two cows remind us of the old principle of common-land, a public place where local cottagers could of right graze their few cattle, sheep or pigs. The creature known as the family pig would alternatively be penned in their own backyard, fattened up, and then sold for slaughter at a modest profit.

38. At one time it was possible to obtain photographic paper
ready designed with a Christmas or other special occasion border design, and a standard postcard backing as approved by the
Post Office, onto which a private snapshot could be printed
ready for posting. An example from about 1912-1915 with a
background of a common in winter.

PARISH CHURCH,
WEST WICKHAM.

39. Though West Wickham Church is virtually timeless as a building, the surroundings look rather different today. The little pond, once grown with reeds and yellow irises, was filled in and grassed over, and much of the approach land behind the righthand trees taken as a carpark. Many of the big trees fell during the 1987 hurricane. The roots of a younger tree (not even planted when this postcard was sent in 1908) dragged up the lychgate's side supports as it fell, causing the whole ancient structure to collapse. Behind the tree second from right is hidden the Lennard Chapel. When in the 1960s Evensong was attracting increasingly large congregations, before the total universality of evening TV, and also of fear of walking to lonely churches at night, the interior vestry was removed to take extra pews, set sideways. A new upstairs vestry was built above the chapel, consecrated by the Bishop of Croydon. A Rector of the 1950s was the last regularly to patrol his parish on horseback.

Wickham Church, KEN

40. A romanticised 'Oilette' type card postmarked 1906, including the lost church pond. Other churches have clearly occupied this site before the present church of 1490, for plaques inside list Rectors back to 1293. More unusually, parish clerks' names are also recorded. Past Rectors included the customary 'painful minister', meaning painstaking rather than a penance to listen to. Within, the chancel structure is noticeably out of line with the cruciform nave and transept; a deliberate distortion representing the drooping of Christ's head on the cross; another very distinct example is the Quire of Canterbury Cathedral. A sanctuary brass commemorates John Lang, a Rector, placed there in 1619, four years before his death. 'At least he was sure of a worthy memorial,' wrote a 1960s church officer. The precious encaustic tiles in the sanctuary, of fleur-de-lys pattern, were laid in 1827, being rediscovered 'loose and neglected'. Estimates of their date range from 14th century to Roman. On a more modern note: St. John's bells were recorded some years ago by the BBC for introducing Sunday morning broadcasts. Their very distinctive timbre was easily recognised by locals whenever they were played over the air.

Church Exterior, West Wickham.

Tanners
Photo Series
9405.

41. Winter at West Wickham in about 1914. The church has since changed little, but its surroundings quite a lot. The rough path has been made up for motor vehicles, though it still ends at the church; and the pond has gone. In its latter days it became considerably overgrown, as rushes, reeds and water irises took hold.

42. West Wickham lychgate was dragged down when this tree fell during the 1987 hurricane, and demolished. When the writer's father Noel Searle was parish clerk, from Coronation Year 1953 to 1971 (as is inscribed on his grave) one of this tower's old bells doubled as a Sanctus bell, which he tolled three times, twice over, during the Consecration at Eucharist. Being dedicated to St. John the Baptist, entry is down steep steps from the tower porch into the nave, commemorating John's prophecy of diminution for himself: 'He must decrease as our Lord increased.' This is seen in many St. John's churches. But Noel Searle's researches showed that the original dedication might have been to St. Mary Magdalene. A charter of 1318 allowed a local fair on her feast day, 22nd July, instead of St. John's Day, 24th June; and fairs nearly always happened on or near the local church's patronal festival. But in 1400, only 82 years after, money was left for a picture of St. John to be installed, suggesting perhaps a new dedication after some rebuilding or refurbishing work.

43. An undated card of St. John's showing the linen-fold carved screen and Agnus Dei (Lamb of God) reredos. As it stood beside Wickham Court, home of Anne Boleyn's aunt, it is assumed that Anne occasionally worshipped here. In 1490 the owner of the Court, Sir Henry Heydon, 'did build a right fair manor place, and a fair church, by Lewisham in Surrey towards Croydon'; such was the widespread local geography of that time. This and previous churches are believed, by now, to have occupied the site for over 900 years. St. John's bells, too, span a long period, from those cast in 1624 and 1640, through to one of 1939. One cracked bell was melted down and recast in 1958. The process was watched at Whitechapel Bell Foundry by some of St. John's staff, one of the local ringers being a director of the works.

44. Churchgoers have been known to nickname Gates Green Road as 'Holy Road', from the number of St. John's staff living in or near it. The old Rectory itself was originally the 17th century Coney Hall Farm, until the 1920s. The cloister-like outbuildings and wonderful old granary behind it, became St. Christopher's Chapel. Being so much used for Sunday School and other children's activities it, too, acquired an appropriate nickname: 'St. Kids' (instead of the usual diminutive for St. Christopher, St. Kits). Inevitably the curate or lay reader in charge has therefore sometimes been unofficially elevated as the 'Bishop of Coney Hall'.

9160. Wickham Court.

45. Wickham Court's intermingled history and legend are too familiar to justify further repetition, but a few lesser known facts and fictions are worth recalling. Stained glass saints in the church next door are said to correspond to old Lennard family names: Anne, Catherine, Christopher, Dorothea. The roof was raised by two feet when in the 1920s it became a hotel, to make the attic rooms lettable. To restore the exterior proportions, the turrets were then raised by ten feet, given new floors, and used for guest bathrooms. 18th century prints show no battlements, which had been removed, but they were restored by the hotel owners. Heraldic glass in one room includes the arms of Anne Boleyn as queen, and also her seal of a white eagle on a tree stump with Tudor rose; the latter was adopted by her daughter Elizabeth I. In the central and now enclosed courtyard was a well for supplying the inhabitants should the Court ever take the role of a castle and come under siege.

46. Rogationtide at St. John's, West Wickham, soon after the Second World War. Leaving only the verger behind 'to watch the shop', the congregation followed the crucifer and choir into the fields for this ancient service of blessing, during Evensong, singing hymns as the walked. One area of the churchyard is popularly called Killick's Corner, from the large number of this family's graves; in particular, Killicks have been local undertakers for many decades. And few men are more jovial off duty than an undertaker, as the writer's family well knows, being close to one of Wickham's church officers. On the other side of the churchyard lies one of the most modest men ever to worship here, buried without any sort of stone or inscription. He believed himself unworthy to be outwardly remembered, compared with the church itself: and God would know where he lay, anyway.

OLD OAKS ON WICKHAM COMMON, KENT.

AFTER THE ORIGINAL PAINTING BY S. JOHNSON.

47. When this postcard titled 'Old Oaks on Wickham Common, Kent' was issued, there was no town; just one straggling hamlet known as Wickham Street, described in about 1875 as 'a pleasant quiet cluster of country cottages about a green, and along the road to Croydon'. This was the same highway that is a madness of cars, lorries and Croydon-bound buses today. A massive tree at its crossroads was the centrepiece, but imagining how it looked, or picturing the general atmosphere, is now very difficult. To gain some idea it is necessary to travel over to still-rural Downe, where a similar monster tree still is the hub of a crossroads, complete with seats wrapped around it. Before suburbia existed, West Wickham was separated from other parishes by open farmland. 'The walks hence... to Beckenham or eastward to Hayes Common, are very beautiful,' it was observed in the 1870s. Today Hayes can still be reached across commonland, but miles of houses lie between Wickham and Beckenham. But even in the 1930s, the author's newlywed parents regulary walked to West Wickham from as far off as Shortlands, entirely across open fields.

48. No mock-Tudor suburbia mars this tranquil scene of about 1905, but the idyll was to last only another twenty years or so. But because the new wave of residents were so enamoured of country life – even though in the process of settling here they were actually destroying it – old style entertainments became very popular. Chief of these was the famous Flitch Trial, run from 1933 to 1941, and again from 1949. On trial were selected local couples whose plea was that they had lived together without one cross word for a year and a day. The winners 'brought home the bacon'. A huge flitch of bacon, weighing sixty pounds, was the 1933 prize, reduced by 1949 to a more manageable joint of bacon airmailed from Canada by a former Wickham resident. Summoned to face trial by jury at the Court of Married Happiness in front of a judge, two counsel, and a jury of six bachelors and six spinsters, each couple was cross questioned in an hilarious spoof of a courtroom trial.

Ham Farm Walk, Beckenham.

49. Where Beckenham, Shirley and West Wickham overlap, their boundaries were once made obscure to the casual eye across one single sweep of green fields. After the 1930s, the same was just as true; but it was now a continuous landscape of semi-detached villas built along innumerable roads with very similar grass verges. Pleasant to live in, but semi-country rather than the real thing. Scenes like Ham Farm Walk had gone for ever.

High Street. West Wickham.

50. Did West Wickham High Street ever really look like this? A scene of about 1905, with only one horse and cart in sight, and a few gracious country houses, when Wickham was little changed from the village of just 884 people described in about 1875 as being 'in the midst of a pleasant and beautiful country, at present not greatly disfigured by the builder'. That sorry stage was not reached until the 1920s and 1930s, when Southern Railway electrification made quick commuting practicable, for ordinary husbands working in London but able to live in the new £400 semis springing up to cash in on this new demand. Miles of countryside were drowned by the resulting sea of suburbia. Even at the period shown, the process was starting at a more moneyed and much slower level, with men like wealthy city bankers and brokers. In 1860, for instance, came the 'spacious castellated mansion' of Monks Orchard on an older house's site, followed by the mock Queen Anne West Wickham House in 1871.

51. A huge visual gulf separates this pre-Great War street in West Wickham, and the inter-wars suburbia succeeding it. During the latter period it teetered between past and future, attaching the word 'village' to events which only marked its transition into a town. Like a 1932 Village Fair raising cash for the site of a new so-called Village Church, because old St. John's was far from the new Wickham. 'The new people who had come to West Wickham to build homes in more pleasant and congenial surroundings, should remember that they... should put proper provision for the service and worship of God,' declared a former Rector. Recent railway electrification had created the outer-suburban commuter, who required value for money, especially when one of them found that season tickets were charged on a fourteen mile journey, though the railway's own timetable put Wickham only 13¼ miles from London, chargeable as thirteen miles. But, craftily, the Southern replied that Charing Cross tickets were also valid on to Cannon Street, making a maximum of just about fourteen miles.

WAR MEMORIAL WEST WICKHAM.

52. West Wickham war memorial when fairly new, standing high on Corkscrew Hill between the medieval and modern Wickhams. In addition to this civic monument, and the unusual Fire Brigade memorial in St. John's churchyard, seven dead of the Second World War were buried in that same ancient God's Acre between January 1942 and February 1945. Apart from Corporal Chudley of the local Home Guard, they were all officers of the RAFVR. A document owned by the author shows that in 1966 the War Graves Commision was paying the church 2s.6d (12½p) a grave 'for annual scrubbing of the war headstones only; i.e., no upkeep of grave space'. This cash was given by the church to the gardener who did this yearly extra job.

53. White Hart Pond was a specially village-like feature of the Surrey end of West Wickham High Street until only a few years ago. It was particulary attractive by night, with the pub's lights reflected in its calm black waters. By day, sadly, it was revealed as more mundane, in deteriorating condition and increasingly used as a dump by the new litter-lout generation. Drained and filled in, it became a mere car park. Because this inn and pond were so near the little Beck Stream (otherwise known as the Ridle or Riddle Brook), this is popularly assumed to be the site of a Wickham mill entered in Domesday Book.

54. The proverbial one-horse-town had its Wickham counterpart: the one-policeman-town. When this card was sent in 1909 it had just appointed a village bobby; in 1929 it still needed only one constable, the same man still pounding the same beat. But when he retired in 1931 it was becoming a sprawling suburb; in the words of a now defunct local paper: 'A builders' paradise... a ratepayers' hell.' The hellish aspect was the failure of everyday facilities to match the enthusiasm of speculative developers for erecting houses. Wickham abounded in booby trap signposts, kerbstones lying around instead of becoming kerbs, muddy puddles, no street lights 'between Dr. Blake's house and the Beckenham boundary', and a stile at a Hawes Lane bridge impossible for the new generation of young suburban mothers to negotiate with prams.

55. Probably this scene was little changed from when a local paper referred to 'this pretty little village' in 1894, as the postcard was written only ten years afterwards. The figures are a reminder of how large families were, ten children being quite common, giving a high juvenile population to such a small community. No less than 270 attended the 1894 Christmas party, split into two events on two separate days. Very predictable gifts were doled out; to the boys: 'Walking sticks, guns, and games', and to the girls 'silk handkerchiefs, vases, dolls, games, workboxes, etc.' Additionally, each child had a shiny new sixpenny (2½ p) piece.

56. The corner by the Fox appears on Keston postcards of all periods, enabling us to chart its various changes. In this one an example of Keston's many public tea gardens is advertised, just beyond the inn. An old wooden signpost points towards Hayes. Down the road is a covered Wild West style freight wagon, suggesting a date before more than a handful of motor vans went on the roads.

57. Keston Fox is readily recognisable, with the lower adjacent block that is now adapted as a Post Office and shop. Opposite is another of Keston's numerous tea gardens, a popular rendez-vous for young men and their sweethearts on a half-day off from the shops and offices of Bromley or Croydon. Outdoor tea and cakes made the perfect cheap prelude to an evening in the 'one-and-nines' (ls.9d or 9p seats at the cinema). Long after the Second World War this tea garden continued, with a children's narrow-gauge railway round the outside edge to attract potential customers' attention as the train rattled past the front fence. Also visible was 'Keston Tunnel' – an old corrugated iron air raid shelter arch – as a reminder of what might have been. Railways were once proposed to serve Keston and Farnborough, as well as the existing Hayes and West Wickham line; had they ever progressed beyond their preliminary enabling acts, all this glorious countryside might have become a Penge-like suburbia.

The Mark, Keston

58. Keston Mark looks somewhat changed today, with its dominant garage on one corner, and certainly no tea shop on the other. On the door of the smaller and lower building is the slogan 'Good Stabling', a reminder that the garage trade had its pre-1920s equivalent. Thus, this has long been a useful crossroads site for trading on travellers, whether putting hay or petrol into their means of transport.

59. Private schools came in all degrees of size and social background. This rather small one at Keston was shown on a postcard in 1910.

60. Areas accepted as 'posh', like Bickley and Keston, were characterised by their private schools, offering education at a fee for gentlemen's sons and daughters, who were not allowed to mingle with ordinary village children for social and snob reasons. This 1910 view shows one of the larger schools, Heathfield. Only just down the road was an equally good example of life at the other end of the scale; tiny cottages known as squats. In the more distant past a family who (by roping in every friend, relation and offspring, and by working as a team for many hours at top speed) could complete an entire cottage and prove its habitability by having a fire lit and smoke coming from the chimney by nightfall, could claim the land they had chosen. A squat's serviceability (as opposed to a ramshackle job merely to acquire a site) is demonstrated by the fact that at least one still survives. Used as a teahouse before the war, it has been modernised and extended into a large bungalow.

61. One of the few compensations of the 1987 hurricane was the opening up of distant views of Holwood House. The loss of giant ornamental trees outside its main frontage lets it stand out from afar and complete many a view from Downe. This is not the house known by the great Prime Minister, Pitt, being rebuilt on or near its site. But the grounds retain many of the trees he knew, and many he would himself have planted.

62. Old Keston pump is said to have been installed 'for the public good' by a local Rector, mindful of the effort of raising water from wells, and of its increasingly poor quality, the source of many a typhoid and cholera outbreak in and around London. A proper drainage grille is visible, preventing a sea of mud and mire around the pump.

Keston

63. The Keston Common cottages in the early 1930s; even today this byway keeps the look of a village. Soon after this card was circulated, the massive stone fountain from outside the Bell in Bromley was removed, after about sixty years on that site, and re-erected here at Keston, in the middle of the grassy space facing the Greyhound, though minus its huge top lantern. It is still there today, complete with some of its bottom plumbing.

64. Keston church, little changed since this postcard was sent in 1905, was described some years before then as 'a humble country church, interesting most from its situation and absence of pretention': far removed from the ostentatious high-Victorian town church of current fashion. Though the writer had little admiration for 'windows altered by the village carpenter and builder', the rest was at least plain and serviceable, 'fitted with high pews, with a row of hat pegs on the walls above'.

65. Wilberforce Oak went through many changes of appearance as mankind fought to preserve it into the 20th century, for its unique associations. A Churchill among trees – the indestructible old warrior toughened instead of bowed by age – it stood for several decades protected behind these iron railings. In the 1950s its deteriorating upper branches, still trying to leaf, were held together by a network of iron braces, struts and rings until time disposed of them. Then a new sapling was put inside the remaining carcase of the giant hollow trunk (though various ramblers have claimed its growth from acorns they spontaneously planted in passing). It flourished for about 35 years until felled in 1987 by Hurricane Len; ironically, the strong young tree collapsed while the original ancient trunk survived, and goes on clinging to life. This card was written in 1908 in conditions that, themselves, are now historic; the dense, dank blanket of fog known as a pea-souper until, following the last and greatest (the Great Smog of 1952), Clean Air Acts consigned those killer vapours to history.

66. Wilberforce Oak in its preserved heyday with some remaining upper branches; today it is reduced to only the split carcase of the bottom trunk. Several generations of ramblers have stopped to read the inscription on the stone Wilberforce Seat, inside its centre medallion. Moved farther back behind the Holwood perimeter fencing for protection from vandalism and other damage, it is much harder now to read. The carved extract from Wilberforce's diary of 1787 runs: 'At length I well remember after a conversation with Mr. Pitt in the open air at the root of an old tree at Holwood, just above the steep descent into the Vale of Keston, I resolved to give notice on a fit occasion in the House of Commons of my intention to bring forward the abolition of the slave trade.'

67. A nice early 20th century example of an extinct type of postcard: the private family snapshot returned from developing in the same format as a commercial view card, with post office approved backing, but printed off one's own negative. This was a popular means of writing to relatives and friends. In this case, a larger portrait was also produced in postcard shape. The marvellous Bernard Shaw style beard belonged to the author's paternal great-grandfather, Alfred Searle, who sits on Wilberforce Seat at utter peace with the world.

68. No amount of scholarly research can scotch the favourite legend of Ceasar's Well. How Ceasar's troops camped at Holwood, weary and thirsty, desperate to find water. And how one sharp-eyed Roman noticed a raven continually returning to one patch of grass as if drinking. Hidden there was a running spring. Hence the name Ceasar's Well for this source of the Ravensbourne: the river or bourne of the raven. It still bubbles up into this circular basin, and flows right across Keston Ponds. Its course is seen as moving water, while the lake around it is almost still. The ponds were created by damming old gravel pits in the 1830s.

KESTON PONDS.

Quch up + write, I will soon   *Yrs G W*

69. Keston Ponds – alternatively known as Keston Lakes – at some uncertain date, looking towards the middle dam.

70. A brief fashion for turning even the most minor springs into miniature spas, cashing in on the heyday of the great and genuine medicinal spas, made even Keston a minor retreat. A pleasant spot for gentle dalliance rather than a non-existent cure. To quote a source of 1792 referring to Ceasar's Well: 'An excellent bath was formed, surrounded by pales and trees'. In 1827 another writer described the well as 'converted into a most useful public cold bath; a dressing house is built on the brink of it; ... and from its romantic situation forms a most pleasing scene'.

71. Keston (anciently Cystaninga or Chestan) had a population of just 717 people not much more than a century ago, and precious few regular links even with the nearest towns of Bromley and Croydon except by horse and cart or the very occasional horse bus. The recommended approach was to tramp all the way, over the lonely Commons: 'a very pleasant walk' if not attacked by what we would now call muggers. A contemporary description reveals that there was no village as such, certainly no central point: 'There is no village proper; a few houses are collected together by the Red Cross Inn, at Keston Mark... a few more by the mill on the Common, where is another country inn, The Fox, and two or three more by the church.' Our view of the Lakes was issued in a book of Bromley area views in about 1892, before the picture postcard era, but the whole series was published in postcard form about ten years later.

POND ON KESTON COMMON, KENT.

AFTER THE ORIGINAL PAINTING BY S. JOHNSON.

72. The Oilette (literally, a little oil painting, specially geared to reproduction in miniature) was much used in Edward VII's period for cards showing simple rural settings. This one is simply inscribed 'Pond on Keston Common, Kent'. When winters were in general longer lasting and more severe than today, Keston Ponds were very popular with people from Bromley and its satellite villages for public skating, directly the ice was thick enough. But nasty accidents often happened when the first signs of thaw set in, and the bravado-brigade ignored warnings that skating was at an end.

ON KESTON COMMON KENT

A.E.SANDERS

73. A gloomy early 20th century view conveying Keston's emptiness off the roads, where only a few horse buses ran through to make it accessible to the public. However, they were gradually improving in frequency, a process begun in the 1860s. In 1869 the well-known Fownes's Keston Omnibus had changed hands, sold to Mr. Lownds of Bromley. The latter then announced 'a first class omnibus service to and from the Bromley station, over Bromley Common to Keston', with what he considered a frequent summer service from April. There was even the prospect of one or two daily buses through Hayes 'should there be a probability of such journeys paying expenses'. Two buses a day: and we now consider a twenty minute wait for a 119 a shameful deterioration in services!

Keston.

3812. 4.

74. An example of a shortlived fashion for spraying glitter onto cards to highlight and decorate them. In this case, shining lines were drawn over the principal tree branches in a winter scene, to simulate frost. The sender was a very precise lady; she dated her card 'Thursday 10.12 pm', meaning twelve minutes past ten in the evening. It obviously caught either a very late post, or a very early morning one, as it is postmarked before nine the next morning.

Keston Common — Kent.

75. Hayes and Keston Commons, one continuous sweep of unspoilt fir, furze and fern, are as lovely now as when a traveller of about 1875 described: 'A broad expanse, high and breezy, bordered by good elms and beech, covered thick with gorse, several varieties of bright coloured heather, wild thyme, harebells and ferns.' Of course, it now lacks 'the Crystal Palace, a conspicuous landmark', as it was totally destroyed by fire in 1936, but 'a mill and groups of red tiled cottages for the sketch book', are still to be found. This undated scene could have been filmed in 1908 (and it probably was), or in 1988, so timeless are the Commons.

76. Another family picture of the type which would be reproduced in both the original snapshot, and as a postcard for mailing to relatives. It shows a tug-of-war in progress on one of the local Commons during a New Church (or Swedenborgian Church) summer outing during the 1920s. Days when pleasures were simple, unsophisticated, taken very near home, and enjoyed as much as the most elaborate overseas tour today.